101 WAYS to EAT COCK

Chicken Cuts
Neck
Back
Wing
Breast
Legs

A Message From

MR. GOOD COCK

There are so many ways to prepare chicken that I thought it made sense to put together a place where you can not only capture all of the amazing recipes that your Mom, family and friends have shared with you over the years, but also the recipes that you have been able to capture from your own trial and error methods.

Sure, I had some fun with the title of the book, but let's be honest, it made you laugh. This is a book that can be passed down from generation to generation in your family to be sure that all of your family recipe secrets are safe for years to come!

Recipe:

Serving:

Prep Time:

Cook Time:

Temperature:

Ingredients:

Methods:

Wine Pairing:

From the Kitchen of:

Recipe:

Serving:

Prep Time:

Cook Time:

Temperature:

Ingredients:

Methods:

Wine Pairing:

From the Kitchen of:

Recipe:

Serving:

Prep Time:

Cook Time:

Temperature:

Ingredients:

Methods:

Wine Pairing:

From the Kitchen of:

Recipe:

Serving:

Prep Time:

Cook Time:

Temperature:

Ingredients:

Methods:

Wine Pairing:

From the Kitchen of:

Recipe:

Serving:

Prep Time:

Cook Time:

Temperature:

Ingredients:

Methods:

Wine Pairing:

From the Kitchen of:

Recipe:

Serving:

Prep Time:

Cook Time:

Temperature:

Ingredients:

Methods:

Wine Pairing:

From the Kitchen of:

Recipe: ______________________

Serving: ____________ Prep Time: ____________

Cook Time: ____________ Temperature: ____________

Ingredients:

Methods:

Wine Pairing: ______________________

From the Kitchen of: ______________________

Recipe:

Serving:

Prep Time:

Cook Time:

Temperature:

Ingredients:

Methods:

Wine Pairing:

From the Kitchen of:

Recipe:

Serving:

Prep Time:

Cook Time:

Temperature:

Ingredients:

Methods:

Wine Pairing:

From the Kitchen of:

Recipe:

Serving:

Prep Time:

Cook Time:

Temperature:

Ingredients:

Methods:

Wine Pairing:

From the Kitchen of:

Recipe:

Serving:

Prep Time:

Cook Time:

Temperature:

Ingredients:

Methods:

Wine Pairing:

From the Kitchen of:

Recipe:

Serving:

Prep Time:

Cook Time:

Temperature:

Ingredients:

Methods:

Wine Pairing:

From the Kitchen of:

Recipe:

Serving:

Prep Time:

Cook Time:

Temperature:

Ingredients:

Methods:

Wine Pairing:

From the Kitchen of:

Recipe:

Serving:

Prep Time:

Cook Time:

Temperature:

Ingredients:

Methods:

Wine Pairing:

From the Kitchen of:

Recipe:

Serving:

Prep Time:

Cook Time:

Temperature:

Ingredients:

Methods:

Wine Pairing:

From the Kitchen of:

Recipe:

Serving:

Prep Time:

Cook Time:

Temperature:

Ingredients:

Methods:

Wine Pairing:

From the Kitchen of:

Recipe: ______________________________

Serving: ______________ Prep Time: ______________

Cook Time: ______________ Temperature: ______________

Ingredients:

Methods:

Wine Pairing: ______________________________

From the Kitchen of: ______________________________

Recipe:

Serving:

Prep Time:

Cook Time:

Temperature:

Ingredients:

Methods:

Wine Pairing:

From the Kitchen of:

Recipe:

Serving:

Prep Time:

Cook Time:

Temperature:

Ingredients:

Methods:

Wine Pairing:

From the Kitchen of:

Recipe:

Serving:

Prep Time:

Cook Time:

Temperature:

Ingredients:

Methods:

Wine Pairing:

From the Kitchen of:

Recipe:

Serving:

Prep Time:

Cook Time:

Temperature:

Ingredients:

Methods:

Wine Pairing:

From the Kitchen of:

Recipe:

Serving:

Prep Time:

Cook Time:

Temperature:

Ingredients:

Methods:

Wine Pairing:

From the Kitchen of:

Recipe:

Serving:

Prep Time:

Cook Time:

Temperature:

Ingredients:

Methods:

Wine Pairing:

From the Kitchen of:

Recipe:

Serving:

Prep Time:

Cook Time:

Temperature:

Ingredients:

Methods:

Wine Pairing:

From the Kitchen of:

Recipe:

Serving:

Prep Time:

Cook Time:

Temperature:

Ingredients:

Methods:

Wine Pairing:

From the Kitchen of:

Recipe:

Serving:

Prep Time:

Cook Time:

Temperature:

Ingredients:

Methods:

Wine Pairing:

From the Kitchen of:

Recipe:

Serving:

Prep Time:

Cook Time:

Temperature:

Ingredients:

Methods:

Wine Pairing:

From the Kitchen of:

Recipe:

Serving:

Prep Time:

Cook Time:

Temperature:

Ingredients:

Methods:

Wine Pairing:

From the Kitchen of:

Recipe:

Serving:

Prep Time:

Cook Time:

Temperature:

Ingredients:

Methods:

Wine Pairing:

From the Kitchen of:

Recipe:

Serving:

Prep Time:

Cook Time:

Temperature:

Ingredients:

Methods:

Wine Pairing:

From the Kitchen of:

Recipe:

Serving:

Prep Time:

Cook Time:

Temperature:

Ingredients:

Methods:

Wine Pairing:

From the Kitchen of:

Recipe:

Serving:

Prep Time:

Cook Time:

Temperature:

Ingredients:

Methods:

Wine Pairing:

From the Kitchen of:

Recipe: ______________________

Serving: ______________ Prep Time: ______________

Cook Time: ______________ Temperature: ______________

Ingredients:

Methods:

Wine Pairing: ______________________

From the Kitchen of: ______________________

Recipe:

Serving:

Prep Time:

Cook Time:

Temperature:

Ingredients:

Methods:

Wine Pairing:

From the Kitchen of:

Recipe:

Serving:

Prep Time:

Cook Time:

Temperature:

Ingredients:

Methods:

Wine Pairing:

From the Kitchen of:

Recipe:

Serving:

Prep Time:

Cook Time:

Temperature:

Ingredients:

Methods:

Wine Pairing:

From the Kitchen of:

Recipe:

Serving:

Prep Time:

Cook Time:

Temperature:

Ingredients:

Methods:

Wine Pairing:

From the Kitchen of:

Recipe:

Serving:

Prep Time:

Cook Time:

Temperature:

Ingredients:

Methods:

Wine Pairing:

From the Kitchen of:

Recipe:

Serving:

Prep Time:

Cook Time:

Temperature:

Ingredients:

Methods:

Wine Pairing:

From the Kitchen of:

Recipe:

Serving:

Prep Time:

Cook Time:

Temperature:

Ingredients:

Methods:

Wine Pairing:

From the Kitchen of:

Recipe:

Serving:

Prep Time:

Cook Time:

Temperature:

Ingredients:

Methods:

Wine Pairing:

From the Kitchen of:

Recipe:

Serving:

Prep Time:

Cook Time:

Temperature:

Ingredients:

Methods:

Wine Pairing:

From the Kitchen of:

Recipe:

Serving:

Prep Time:

Cook Time:

Temperature:

Ingredients:

Methods:

Wine Pairing:

From the Kitchen of:

Recipe:

Serving:

Prep Time:

Cook Time:

Temperature:

Ingredients:

Methods:

Wine Pairing:

From the Kitchen of:

Recipe:

Serving:

Prep Time:

Cook Time:

Temperature:

Ingredients:

Methods:

Wine Pairing:

From the Kitchen of:

Recipe:

Serving:

Prep Time:

Cook Time:

Temperature:

Ingredients:

Methods:

Wine Pairing:

From the Kitchen of:

Recipe:

Serving:

Prep Time:

Cook Time:

Temperature:

Ingredients:

Methods:

Wine Pairing:

From the Kitchen of:

Recipe: ____________________

Serving: ____________________ Prep Time: ____________________

Cook Time: ____________________ Temperature: ____________________

Ingredients:

Methods:

Wine Pairing: ____________________

From the Kitchen of: ____________________

Recipe:

Serving:

Prep Time:

Cook Time:

Temperature:

Ingredients:

Methods:

Wine Pairing:

From the Kitchen of:

Recipe:

Serving:

Prep Time:

Cook Time:

Temperature:

Ingredients:

Methods:

Wine Pairing:

From the Kitchen of:

Recipe:

Serving:

Prep Time:

Cook Time:

Temperature:

Ingredients:

Methods:

Wine Pairing:

From the Kitchen of:

Recipe:

Serving:

Prep Time:

Cook Time:

Temperature:

Ingredients:

Methods:

Wine Pairing:

From the Kitchen of:

Recipe:

Serving:

Prep Time:

Cook Time:

Temperature:

Ingredients:

Methods:

Wine Pairing:

From the Kitchen of:

Recipe:

Serving:

Prep Time:

Cook Time:

Temperature:

Ingredients:

Methods:

Wine Pairing:

From the Kitchen of:

Recipe:

Serving:

Prep Time:

Cook Time:

Temperature:

Ingredients:

Methods:

Wine Pairing:

From the Kitchen of:

Recipe:

Serving:

Prep Time:

Cook Time:

Temperature:

Ingredients:

Methods:

Wine Pairing:

From the Kitchen of:

Recipe:

Serving:

Prep Time:

Cook Time:

Temperature:

Ingredients:

Methods:

Wine Pairing:

From the Kitchen of:

Recipe:

Serving:

Prep Time:

Cook Time:

Temperature:

Ingredients:

Methods:

Wine Pairing:

From the Kitchen of:

Recipe:

Serving:

Prep Time:

Cook Time:

Temperature:

Ingredients:

Methods:

Wine Pairing:

From the Kitchen of:

Recipe:

Serving:

Prep Time:

Cook Time:

Temperature:

Ingredients:

Methods:

Wine Pairing:

From the Kitchen of:

Recipe:

Serving:

Prep Time:

Cook Time:

Temperature:

Ingredients:

Methods:

Wine Pairing:

From the Kitchen of:

Recipe:

Serving:

Prep Time:

Cook Time:

Temperature:

Ingredients:

Methods:

Wine Pairing:

From the Kitchen of:

Recipe: ______________________________

Serving: ______________ Prep Time: ______________

Cook Time: ______________ Temperature: ______________

Ingredients:

Methods:

Wine Pairing: ______________________________

From the Kitchen of: ______________________________

Recipe:

Serving:

Prep Time:

Cook Time:

Temperature:

Ingredients:

Methods:

Wine Pairing:

From the Kitchen of:

Recipe: ______________________________

Serving: ______________ Prep Time: ______________

Cook Time: ______________ Temperature: ______________

Ingredients:

Methods:

Wine Pairing: ______________________________

From the Kitchen of: ______________________________

Recipe:

Serving:

Prep Time:

Cook Time:

Temperature:

Ingredients:

Methods:

Wine Pairing:

From the Kitchen of:

Recipe:

Serving:

Prep Time:

Cook Time:

Temperature:

Ingredients:

Methods:

Wine Pairing:

From the Kitchen of:

Recipe:

Serving:

Prep Time:

Cook Time:

Temperature:

Ingredients:

Methods:

Wine Pairing:

From the Kitchen of:

Recipe:

Serving:

Prep Time:

Cook Time:

Temperature:

Ingredients:

Methods:

Wine Pairing:

From the Kitchen of:

Recipe:

Serving:

Prep Time:

Cook Time:

Temperature:

Ingredients:

Methods:

Wine Pairing:

From the Kitchen of:

Recipe:

Serving:

Prep Time:

Cook Time:

Temperature:

Ingredients:

Methods:

Wine Pairing:

From the Kitchen of:

Recipe:

Serving:

Prep Time:

Cook Time:

Temperature:

Ingredients:

Methods:

Wine Pairing:

From the Kitchen of:

Recipe:

Serving:

Prep Time:

Cook Time:

Temperature:

Ingredients:

Methods:

Wine Pairing:

From the Kitchen of:

Recipe:

Serving:

Prep Time:

Cook Time:

Temperature:

Ingredients:

Methods:

Wine Pairing:

From the Kitchen of:

Recipe:

Serving:

Prep Time:

Cook Time:

Temperature:

Ingredients:

Methods:

Wine Pairing:

From the Kitchen of:

Recipe:

Serving:

Prep Time:

Cook Time:

Temperature:

Ingredients:

Methods:

Wine Pairing:

From the Kitchen of:

Recipe:

Serving:

Prep Time:

Cook Time:

Temperature:

Ingredients:

Methods:

Wine Pairing:

From the Kitchen of:

Recipe:

Serving:

Prep Time:

Cook Time:

Temperature:

Ingredients:

Methods:

Wine Pairing:

From the Kitchen of:

Recipe:

Serving:

Prep Time:

Cook Time:

Temperature:

Ingredients:

Methods:

Wine Pairing:

From the Kitchen of:

Recipe:

Serving:

Prep Time:

Cook Time:

Temperature:

Ingredients:

Methods:

Wine Pairing:

From the Kitchen of:

Recipe:

Serving:

Prep Time:

Cook Time:

Temperature:

Ingredients:

Methods:

Wine Pairing:

From the Kitchen of:

Recipe:

Serving:

Prep Time:

Cook Time:

Temperature:

Ingredients:

Methods:

Wine Pairing:

From the Kitchen of:

Recipe:

Serving:

Prep Time:

Cook Time:

Temperature:

Ingredients:

Methods:

Wine Pairing:

From the Kitchen of:

Recipe:

Serving:

Prep Time:

Cook Time:

Temperature:

Ingredients:

Methods:

Wine Pairing:

From the Kitchen of:

Recipe:

Serving:

Prep Time:

Cook Time:

Temperature:

Ingredients:

Methods:

Wine Pairing:

From the Kitchen of:

Recipe:

Serving:

Prep Time:

Cook Time:

Temperature:

Ingredients:

Methods:

Wine Pairing:

From the Kitchen of:

Recipe:

Serving:

Prep Time:

Cook Time:

Temperature:

Ingredients:

Methods:

Wine Pairing:

From the Kitchen of:

Recipe:

Serving:

Prep Time:

Cook Time:

Temperature:

Ingredients:

Methods:

Wine Pairing:

From the Kitchen of:

Recipe:

Serving:

Prep Time:

Cook Time:

Temperature:

Ingredients:

Methods:

Wine Pairing:

From the Kitchen of:

Recipe:

Serving:

Prep Time:

Cook Time:

Temperature:

Ingredients:

Methods:

Wine Pairing:

From the Kitchen of:

Recipe:

Serving:

Prep Time:

Cook Time:

Temperature:

Ingredients:

Methods:

Wine Pairing:

From the Kitchen of:

Recipe:

Serving:

Prep Time:

Cook Time:

Temperature:

Ingredients:

Methods:

Wine Pairing:

From the Kitchen of:

Recipe:

Serving:

Prep Time:

Cook Time:

Temperature:

Ingredients:

Methods:

Wine Pairing:

From the Kitchen of:

Recipe:

Serving:

Prep Time:

Cook Time:

Temperature:

Ingredients:

Methods:

Wine Pairing:

From the Kitchen of:

Recipe:

Serving:

Prep Time:

Cook Time:

Temperature:

Ingredients:

Methods:

Wine Pairing:

From the Kitchen of:

Recipe:

Serving:

Prep Time:

Cook Time:

Temperature:

Ingredients:

Methods:

Wine Pairing:

From the Kitchen of:

Recipe:

Serving:

Prep Time:

Cook Time:

Temperature:

Ingredients:

Methods:

Wine Pairing:

From the Kitchen of:

Recipe:

Serving:

Prep Time:

Cook Time:

Temperature:

Ingredients:

Methods:

Wine Pairing:

From the Kitchen of:

Recipe:

Serving:

Prep Time:

Cook Time:

Temperature:

Ingredients:

Methods:

Wine Pairing:

From the Kitchen of:

Recipe:

Serving:

Prep Time:

Cook Time:

Temperature:

Ingredients:

Methods:

Wine Pairing:

From the Kitchen of:

Recipe: ______

Serving: ______ Prep Time: ______

Cook Time: ______ Temperature: ______

Ingredients:

Methods:

Wine Pairing: ______

From the Kitchen of: ______

Printed in Great Britain
by Amazon

68530978R00061